A Discovery Biography

Clara Barton

— ◆ —

Soldier of Mercy

by **Mary Catherine Rose**
illustrated by E. Harper Johnson

CHELSEA JUNIORS
A division of Chelsea House Publishers
New York • Philadelphia

The Discovery Biographies have been prepared under the
educational supervision of Mary C. Austin, Ed.D.,
Reading Specialist and Professor of Education, Case
Western Reserve University.

Cover illustration: Eileen McKeating

First Chelsea House edition 1991

1 3 5 7 9 8 6 4 2

ISBN   0-7910-1403-7

Contents

Clara Barton:

Soldier of Mercy

	Page
CHAPTER 1	
Christmas Cookies	7
CHAPTER 2	
Too Many Teachers	13
CHAPTER 3	
Off to School	19
CHAPTER 4	
The Little Nurse	25
CHAPTER 5	
The Ball Game	31
CHAPTER 6	
Off to War	39
CHAPTER 7	
A Narrow Escape	47
CHAPTER 8	
Missing Soldiers	55
CHAPTER 9	
A New Flag	61
CHAPTER 10	
The American Red Cross . . .	69
CHAPTER 11	
Christmas Day	75

Chapter *1*

Christmas Cookies

It was Christmas morning in 1824. All night soft snow had fallen on the small white farmhouse in eastern Massachusetts.

The five Barton children stood by the fireplace in the big front room. They had all opened their presents except Clara, the youngest. Their mother did not believe in dolls and toys. So only a few packages lay under the tree.

"Let's watch Clara open her present," said Dorothy, the oldest sister.

"It's something red," said Clara. She pulled off the wrapping paper. "Oh, what pretty mittens! And I love the color red!"

"Merry Christmas, Happy Birthday, little one," laughed her big brother, Stephen. He picked her up and pretended to groan. "Oh — you're getting too heavy for me!"

"I'm three years old today," Clara said proudly. "I'm a big girl now."

Actually, Clara was very small, even for her age. All her life she was a tiny person.

Clara was the baby of the family. Her birthday was on Christmas day.

So she had a special package. It was a box of sugar cookies.

Clara looked at the cookies with hungry eyes. But she was a generous little girl. She wanted to share her treat.

"Line up, and I will give everyone some cookies," Clara told her family. "Father and Mother first —"

Brothers and sisters came next. The last in line was Buttons, Clara's little dog. He was all white with dark brown eyes. He could sit up and beg and could do other tricks.

Clara went down the line. She gave each one a few of her cookies. But when she came to the end, her hands were empty.

"Clara has given away too much," her mother said. "She has no cookies left for herself. We'll each give her back some. Then she will have her share."

Little Clara went down the line again. Her mother and father each gave her some cookies back. The brothers and sisters gave her some too. But Buttons had already gobbled up his share.

Clara looked at Buttons. She shook her head. "Buttons, you were not *polite*," she said sadly.

Chapter *2*

Too Many Teachers

Clara was twelve years younger than any of her sisters and brothers. When they were at school, she missed them. She had to play alone. There were no neighbors near the Barton farm.

In warm weather she played tea-party on the wide front doorstep. She poured tea in pink and white china cups. Faithful Buttons was her guest.

In winter Clara played by the warm stove in the big kitchen. Her two older sisters were teachers. They taught Clara to read before she was old enough to go to school. She was not so lonely when she could read storybooks to herself. She also drew pictures and cut out paper dolls.

Clara's older brother Stephen was an arithmetic teacher. He showed Clara how to add and subtract numbers on her slate.

David was another of Clara's brothers. He gave her a very different kind of lessons. He loved horses and outdoor games. David taught Clara to play ball. He showed her how to pitch a ball hard and straight and how to run fast.

He gave Clara horseback riding lessons.

"He taught me to ride a lively horse bareback," Clara remembered later. "Then he got on another horse and off we would gallop, over the fields. I had to hold tight to my horse's mane!"

"You must learn to ride anything on four legs," David told the little girl.

Clara's mother taught her to cook and bake and sew. Her father had been a captain in the French and Indian wars. He lined up toy soldiers on the parlor floor to show Clara how soldiers fought battles. He told her stories about war and battles. Clara liked this best of all.

The little girl sighed. "I wish *I* could be a soldier."

Clara's father taught her the names of all the presidents and vice-presidents of the United States. One of her older sisters discovered that Clara thought presidents must be much bigger than other people.

"A president is as tall as a church steeple," Clara said solemnly. "A vice-president is only as tall as the school-house."

Mrs. Barton laughed. But she shook her head. "No little girl ever had so many teachers as Clara," she said. "No wonder she is confused."

Clara's family was very proud of her. "When she goes to school she will be the best pupil," they said.

Chapter *3*

Off to School

When Clara was almost four years old, her parents let her go to school. One cold winter day her big brother Stephen put Clara on his shoulders. He carried her through the deep snow to the school.

Clara was a shy little girl. She was frightened by people she did not know. She wasn't sure she would like school.

Stephen comforted her. "It's a one-room school, little one," he told Clara.

"All the classes do their lessons in the same room. There will be lots of children for you to play with."

But Clara was frightened when she saw so many strangers. She wanted to cry. "Please take me home, Stephen," she begged. "I'm afraid."

"No, you must stay," her brother said gently. "Make us proud of you!"

The little girl slowly took off her coat. She found a seat near the front of the room where the smaller children sat. Clara looked around timidly and wished she were any place but there.

Clara did her work well. But she was often afraid to talk in school. She thought the other children might laugh at her.

As soon as school was over, she ran to her brothers and sisters. Clara was never really happy at school.

Clara's parents were worried. "If we sent Clara away to boarding school, perhaps she would make friends more easily," they said.

Clara went away to school. Her father took her on the journey. He put her trunk in the buggy beside her. Clara was unhappy. A boarding school was a place where children lived while they went to school. Clara only wanted to live at home.

"We Bartons are always brave," Clara's father said, when he left her. *"When there is something we must do, we do it!"*

Clara felt sad. "I'll try," she said.

But the school seemed terribly big to the little girl. The table where the pupils ate seemed too long. It wasn't like the family table at home.

Clara did well in her studies. The teachers were kind to her.

But she was still unhappy. She could not eat or sleep.

Before long, Clara's father came to take her home. "We sent her away too soon," Clara's father said. "Later on she will learn not to be afraid."

Clara packed her trunk and rode back with her father. She was glad to be going home. But she thought she had failed because she had not stayed at school. She hoped she could learn to be more brave.

Later in her life Clara Barton was called the bravest woman in America. When she found something she really wanted to do, she did it.

"But I never got over being afraid of strangers," Clara Barton wrote. "I would rather face a cannon than make a speech to a roomful of strange people."

Chapter *4*

The Little Nurse

When Clara was eleven years old something happened that changed her whole life. It began when her father decided he needed a new barn.

"Tomorrow the neighbors will come to help your father build his new barn," Clara's mother said one day. "The men will work on the barn. The women will cook and visit, and the children can play. It will be like a big party."

The next morning Clara walked down
to the place where the men were working. She watched David climb the
ladder to the top of the new barn.
"What a big, strong brother I have!"
Clara thought. "How brave he looks
standing on that long board so high
above the ground!"

Suddenly the board broke and David
fell crashing to the ground. Everyone
ran to help him.

"I'm all right," David said, standing
up. "I wasn't hurt."

But later than night David's head
began to ache. He had a high fever.
When the doctor came, Clara waited
outside David's door.

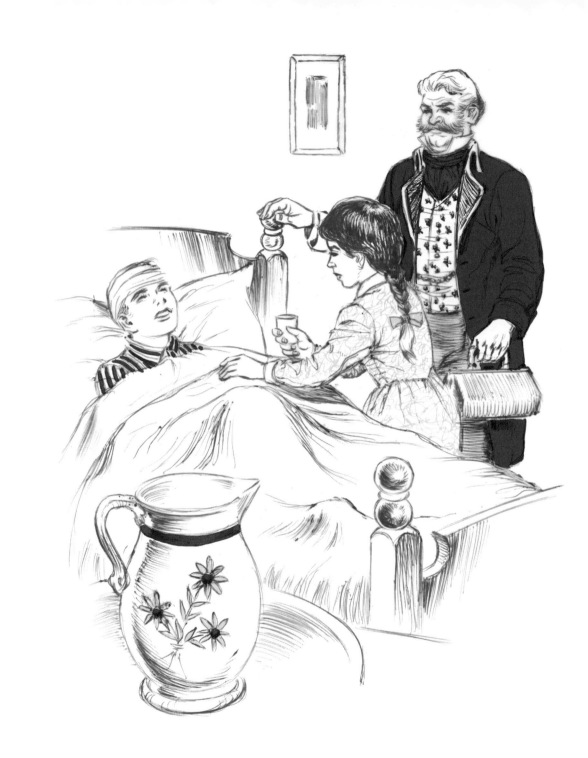

"He won't let anyone come near him," Clara heard her mother say. "Poor boy. He is in such pain."

"Please, Mother," Clara begged. "Let me see David. Let me try to help him."

"All right, child, but only for a few minutes," her mother said.

Clara went into the room. David had always been so strong. Now he lay still. His face was white. His eyes were closed.

The doctor was afraid David would die. But Clara was sure she could make him well. She begged to be his nurse. The doctor showed Clara how to give David his medicine and take care of him. For many months Clara worked day and night to help her brother get well.

The only "playing" she did during the long months was to go for short rides on her horse. Her older sisters helped her do her school work at home.

No matter how sick David was, Clara never lost hope.

"I won't give up," Clara told her brother over and over. "You *will* get well. I *know* you will!"

It was a wonderful day for Clara when David finally walked out of his room and into the sunshine.

"It was my little nurse who made me get well," David told everyone.

The doctor agreed. "The child is a natural nurse," he told Clara's mother and father.

Clara's father had given her a beautiful horse named Billy. While David was sick, Clara did not have time to ride Billy. Now Clara and David could ride together once again. They had such fun! Then Clara had a new wish.

She hoped that when she was grown up she could help other people as she had helped David.

This wish became the most important thing in Clara's life. She wanted to help people all over the world.

"If only I can find the way to help," she thought.

Chapter *5*

The Ball Game

It was a cold fall day several years later. Clara sat indoors by a warm fire. Suddenly she overheard her mother talking to a friend in the next room. "Our Clara is shy and afraid to meet people," Mrs. Barton was saying. "Do you know of anything we can do to help her?"

"I don't think she will ever learn to stand up for herself," said the friend.

"But she is not afraid to speak up for other people. She should find something to do where she can help others. Then she will forget to be afraid." The friend was quiet a moment. Then he said, "Perhaps Clara should become a school-teacher."

"A teacher," Clara whispered to herself. "That would be a way to help others!" She turned the idea over in her mind. Then she said firmly, "Yes, that's what I will do. I will be a teacher, and a good one, too!"

A few months later Clara Barton put up her hair and lengthened her skirts. She was only in her teens and still very small for her age. She wanted to look older when she took her first job. In those days people did not need any special training to become teachers. So Clara had to teach a class without anyone to tell her just what to do.

On the first day of school, Clara was more frightened than ever. Some of the boys were bigger than she was. She saw them wink at each other and whisper behind their hands. "The boys made so much trouble for the last teacher that she had to leave," Clara thought. "How can I ever make them behave? What will I do with them?"

Somehow she got through the first day, and the second. Then the next day there was a fight during the lunch hour. The boys were quarreling over a ball game.

Clara went to help. "You are playing this game all wrong," she said. "You haven't learned the rules. Give me the ball. I'll pitch."

The boys laughed. In those days, girls did not play boys' games. Moreover, their new teacher was very small. She didn't weigh even one hundred pounds.

But Clara remembered how David had taught her to throw a ball, hard and straight. And she could run the bases faster than the boys.

The big boys stopped laughing when they saw Clara play. How surprised they were to find their teacher could pitch and run better than they could.

"Bless David for teaching me to play ball," Clara whispered to herself.

She played many other games with the children. The boys didn't laugh at her again. They were proud of their teacher. They knew she was their friend.

Clara enjoyed teaching school. She made her children enjoy school too. She seemed to forget her shyness when she was thinking of the children.

Clara became known as a fine teacher. She was sent to different schools where there had been trouble with the older pupils. When she came, the trouble soon disappeared.

She worked every day from early morning until late at night. She became very tired. One morning Clara found that she could not talk. She could only whisper.

"You have worked too hard," her
doctor said. "You must take a long
rest."

Chapter *6*

Off to War

Clara Barton decided to go to Washington, the nation's capital, for a change and rest. But she was not still for long.

"I'm *tired* of resting," she soon told her friends. "I want to find a job."

Clara found a job in Washington. She was one of the first women to work in a government office.

In her free time, Clara went to hear the speakers in Congress. She was interested in the debates. At this time the congressmen from the North and the South were not able to agree about many important matters. Most of all, they argued about the right to own slaves. Finally, in 1861, a war between the Northern States and the Southern States began.

After the battles started, many of the wounded men were sent back to Washington for care. For there were no hospitals and few doctors at the battlefront. Some wounded soldiers were taken care of in hospital tents near the lines. But most of them waited days to be helped. They were brought many miles in wagons over rough roads. On the long journey to the hospitals the wounded men had no medicine to help

their pain. There were no nurses to take care of them. Many times they had no food.

How badly they needed someone to nurse them! She remembered what she had said to her father when she was a little girl. "I wish *I* could be a soldier."

Now Clara Barton had an idea. "If I can't be a soldier, I want to *help* soldiers," she said. "I can be a new kind of soldier. There is no one on the battlefields to help the wounded men.

And often there are not enough medicines or bandages. The men would have
a much better chance of getting well if
they could get help sooner."

As soon as Clara got home from work
one night she started writing letters.
She wrote to her relatives and friends.
She asked them to help her. "If I can
get money for supplies of food and
medicines, I will take them right to the
battlefields to help our soldiers," she
wrote. Her friends were generous. Soon
she had a warehouse full of food and
blankets and bandages.

Clara went to see some of the generals
of the Northern Army. She asked them
to let her go to the battlefront.

There were no "trained" nurses at

that time. Women learned to nurse by helping their sick friends and families, just as Clara had done.

"Give me a chance," Clara begged the generals. "Let me go to the battle-fields. I can keep many of your men from dying."

The generals did not think the battle-field was the right place for a woman. "No woman would know what to do in war," they said.

Clara remembered her father's stories of his army days. "I will know what to do," she said. "Just let me go."

At last a general said to Clara, "Our wounded men do need help on the battlefield, Miss Barton. You are the one to give it to them. We will give you a wagon for your supplies."

Later the Northern Army gave Clara money for more supplies. They gave her a whole train of army wagons, and men to load them. Her wish to help others had really come true.

Chapter 7

A Narrow Escape

Clara Barton was allowed to travel about freely on the battlefields. She could go when and where she pleased.

One day she saw rows of wounded men lying on the bare ground in front of a hospital. They were waiting for the busy doctors to see them.

Clara stopped to help feed the men. She tried to find extra coats and blankets for the ones who were most badly hurt.

Clara leaned over one soldier. His eyes were closed.

"Try to take a little soup," she said gently. "It will help you."

The man swallowed. Then he opened his eyes and looked up. "Thank you, Miss Barton," he said weakly.

Clara was startled. Then she recognized the weak voice. The bearded soldier was one of the boys she had taught in school. He was in a group of soldiers from Massachusetts. Clara looked around. She found some of her other pupils, and some of her neighbors from home. Many of them were weak and dying because they had been so long without food or care. Clara stayed to help the men until they entered the hospital.

On one of her trips to the battlefront, Clara looked at the most dreadful sight she had ever seen. There were three thousand wounded men lying on the bare ground waiting for help — her help!

Without a moment's delay Clara began building a fire, preparing food, and bandaging wounds. She seemed to be everywhere at once. She worked all day and through the night.

When there were no blankets left, Clara covered the men with hay to keep them warm.

When daylight came, a young officer rode up. He pointed to a cloud of cannon smoke. "The enemy will soon be here, Miss Barton!" he warned her. "You will not be safe here when the

fighting starts. Please leave at once."

Clara saw some wounded men still waiting to be put in wagons. "There are men here who need me. I cannot go yet," she replied quietly.

Clara hurried to finish her work. She saw that all the men were put safely into wagons, or on the train. They would be taken to hospitals.

The young officer came back. "Hurry, Miss Barton," he said, pointing to enemy soldiers rushing over the hill. "Take my horse and ride to the train. If you ride fast, you can still get on it!"

The horse bucked and reared, but Clara held on tightly. The train was already moving slowly. Her horse galloped beside it.

A man on the train saw Clara. He held out his hand. *"Jump,"* he shouted.

Clara kicked her feet free. She reached for the man's hand and jumped to the train. Her horse galloped away, and Clara sank into the train car with a sigh of relief. None of the wounded soldiers had been left behind. They were safe. She had escaped. Now she was safe too.

"Bless David again," Clara whispered, "for teaching me to ride *anything on four legs!"*

Chapter *8*

Missing Soldiers

Clara Barton was forty-four when the Civil War ended. She had followed "her soldiers" for almost four years. She was a soldier herself, a soldier of mercy bringing help to the suffering.

Somehow Clara found out where many of the battles were taking place. She would rush her supplies to the field. She was everywhere doing everything.

Other nurses had followed her to the battlefront. But Clara was the most famous. She cared for the wounded men. She comforted them and wrote letters home for them.

Once when someone wished for an apple pie, Clara stayed up all night making ninety apple pies. The grateful soldiers called her the "angel of the battlefield."

When the war ended, Clara Barton returned to Washington. She opened her door and almost fell over a large basket filled with letters. Some of the letters were to welcome her home. Some were from her family. But most of them were from people who wanted to find their sons or fathers or uncles who were missing in the war.

They did not know whether their loved ones were dead, or just too sick to write.

Tired as she was, Clara read each letter carefully. She knew the answers to a few, and wrote to the worried families. Then she sent names of the missing men to towns all over the country. She asked everyone who knew anything about a missing soldier to write her. Other worried families heard of what Clara was doing. Soon she got almost a hundred letters each day.

Clara visited Abraham Lincoln, the President of the United States. "Miss Barton," he said, "you are doing a fine work. Please go on. The country will give you money." He promised her help from the government.

Still there was not enough money. How could she get more? "Why don't you give talks about your work in the war?" a friend suggested. "Lots of people would pay to hear you."

"I would be afraid to stand before so many people," Clara Barton thought. "But if I want to go on with my work of finding missing soldiers, I must forget about being afraid."

So she traveled about, telling of her nursing work in the war. She learned not to show that she was afraid.

Clara spent four years searching for missing men. She went through old hospital and prison records. She wrote thousands of families telling them their sons or brothers or husbands were found.

Finally the work was too much for her. One night she smiled at her audience. She opened her mouth to speak, but no sound came. Her voice was gone again.

"You must have a complete rest," her doctor told her. "Go to another country and have a real vacation."

Chapter *9*

A New Flag

Clara Barton went across the ocean to Switzerland. She loved the lakes and the high, snow-covered mountains. But, as usual, Clara did not rest long.

For soon she met Dr. Appia, a leader in the Red Cross work which had just been started in Europe. He visited Clara and told her about the Red Cross.

He explained that it had been started so that wounded soldiers could get help in wartime.

"There are twenty-two countries that have joined the Red Cross," said Dr. Appia. "The twenty-two countries are friendly. But if the countries should ever go to war against each other, they have promised to obey the Red Cross rules. They promise not to shoot at medical workers, or at hospitals or medical supply trains. And they will help *any* wounded men — their own soldiers and enemy soldiers as well. They also promise to give food and clothes and medical care to families who might be homeless or hurt because of the fighting."

If all countries obeyed the Red Cross rules, wounded soldiers could get help quickly no matter where they were. Dr. Appia wanted the United States to join

the Red Cross. He hoped Clara Barton
would help get them to join.

"Dr. Appia," Clara promised, "I will
write to friends in America and tell
them about the Red Cross. And when
I return, I will do more to help."

Soon Clara had a chance to see the Red Cross in action. A war started in Germany and she went to help. She was amazed to see the many supplies and the nurses the Red Cross had trained. She decided to spend the rest of her life working for the Red Cross.

When the war was over, she stayed on in Germany. The war had destroyed many people's homes and often left them without jobs or money.

"These people need work so they can get food and clothing," Clara told a friend. "A sewing room would give them clothes to wear and jobs to do!" Clara started a sewing room with her own money.

Later, when Clara returned to America, she was sick for a long time. But she did not forget the Red Cross. As soon as she was well, Clara went to Washington. Most people she talked to felt that the United States did not need the Red Cross. "It would be useful in wartime," they said, "but our country is not at war."

Clara was disappointed, but she never gave up.

"Our country is at peace," Clara said. "We pray it always will be. But even in peace time there are enemies to fight all over the world. The enemies of nature — floods and fires, earthquakes, famines and sickness."

Clara talked with many different presidents and government leaders over the years. But all she was able to do was to start a few Red Cross groups in New York state.

Finally a terrible forest fire in Michigan showed the American people how useful the Red Cross could be. As soon as Clara read about the fires, she knew that many families in Michigan would be homeless and hungry. She and her workers from New York packed up all the food, clothes and blankets they could find and rushed them to Michigan.

All the newspapers wrote about Clara's work in Michigan. It had taken her thirteen years to show Americans how much good the Red Cross could do.

In 1882 the United States joined the other nations in the Red Cross. At last Clara saw the white flag, with its red cross, fly against the blue sky. Clara Barton was very proud. All her life she had been a soldier of mercy. This was the flag of mercy.

Chapter *10*

The American Red Cross

Clara Barton was made the first President of the American Red Cross. She was sixty-one years old, but no one would have guessed her age. Her hair was still dark and her eyes were bright. She loved her work and this kept her young and strong.

One of the first disasters to which the American Red Cross sent help was the Ohio River flood. During the flood, houses and entire families were swept away by the swift flood waters. Clara left the Red Cross headquarters in Washington and hurried to Ohio. She rented a boat and had it filled with food, clothes and coal. Then she and her Red Cross workers traveled up and down the river helping homeless people.

She did not forget the animals. Often she saw horses, cows, sheep and pigs standing on small pieces of land with water around them. Clara was rowed out and she fed the animals herself.

"Our workers were kept busy for months," said Clara. "We even got boards and nails and helped people build new homes."

For twenty-two years, Clara Barton worked for the Red Cross. She traveled all over the United States and in many other countries too.

At the time of the Spanish-American War, Clara was seventy-six. Yet she went to Cuba and slept in an army tent. She even rode to the battlefield in an army wagon filled with supplies.

When the soldiers saw her, they shouted, "Here comes the Red Cross!" "Here's Clara Barton!" "Now we'll get something to eat!"

"It is like the terrible days of the Civil War all over again," Clara thought. She saw the wounded soldiers lying on the wet ground. Clara soon had a fire going and food cooking.

A doctor who worked with Clara said,
"Miss Barton is wonderful. She is a tiny
woman, but the biggest, roughest soldiers
always obey her. She is stronger than
any of us. She can work all day and
all night. She never stops when there's
a job to be done!"

Years later, Clara told of Colonel Theodore Roosevelt's visit to the Red Cross camp in Cuba. He had come to buy supplies for his wounded men.

"I'm sorry, sir, but we cannot sell hospital supplies," she told him.

"But my men need these things," he insisted. "How can I get them?"

"Just ask for them, Colonel. The Red Cross is happy to *give* to those in need!"

A smile brightened his face. Soon he was on his way with the things he needed.

With Clara to guide it, the Red Cross grew large and strong. "Wherever help is needed," Clara Barton said, "the Red Cross must be there."

Chapter *11*

Christmas Day

In 1904 Clara Barton was eighty-three. She resigned as President of the American Red Cross. But it was hard for her to sit still, doing nothing. She wrote books, went to meetings, and made speeches. She organized the National First Aid Association.

The next few years were busy ones. Clara often visited her home town in

Massachusetts. She enjoyed seeing her great-nieces and nephews. Her favorite nephew, Stephen, was often in Washington. He had been one of her most important helpers in Red Cross work.

Stephen sometimes visited her at her country house near Washington, D. C.

"You should call this Adventure House, Auntie," Stephen said.

"It is an interesting house," Clara agreed, "and I enjoy taking care of it." Clara did her own cooking and cleaning. She washed and ironed.

"I've always liked to work," Clara told her friends. "Why should I change my ways now?" She fed her chickens and her pigs. She planted her garden and took care of her favorite horse, Baba.

Christmas had always been a very special day for Clara Barton. One Christmas, near the end of her life, Clara lighted the fire in her parlor and put her favorite Christmas cards across the mantelpiece. Baskets were filled with cards and messages from all over the world. She had presents from her friends and family.

Clara looked about the house. "My life has been *adventure*," she thought. "I am lucky to have come home safely."

The flags of the Red Cross nations where she had worked hung in the big hall. There were books and paintings and souvenirs from all her travels. Best of all, there were the many decorations and medals Clara Barton had received for her work.

As Clara sat by the fire, there was a loud knock on the front door. She went to answer it.

"Merry Christmas! Happy Birthday!" shouted many voices, young and old.

There in her doorway stood Clara Barton's neighbors and their children.

"What a wonderful surprise! Come in! Come in!" she said.

Clara found it hard to believe so many people had remembered her birthday. "What a lucky thing that I baked Christmas cookies this morning," she said. "You must all have some!"

"Thank you, Miss Red Cross!" said a little boy as he took a cookie.

Everyone laughed. It was a good name for Clara Barton.

When the children and their parents had gone home, the house was quiet again.

"What a merry Christmas," Clara thought. "What a happy birthday!"

She went upstairs and put her lamp in the window. It shone out across the snow into the cold, dark night.

The memory of Clara Barton still shines through the whole world today. Wherever the Red Cross flag flies, the spirit of Clara Barton, the shy little girl who became a brave woman, flies with it.